KIPPUR

illustrations by Ayala Gordon

United Synagogue Commission on Jewish Education

Copyright © 1959 by United Synagogue of America · Printed in U.S.A.

After Rosh Hashanah
  comes Yom Kippur,
    the second High Holiday.
Daddy comes home early,
  while the sun is high in the sky.

יוֹם כִּפּוּר

YOM

by Norma Simon

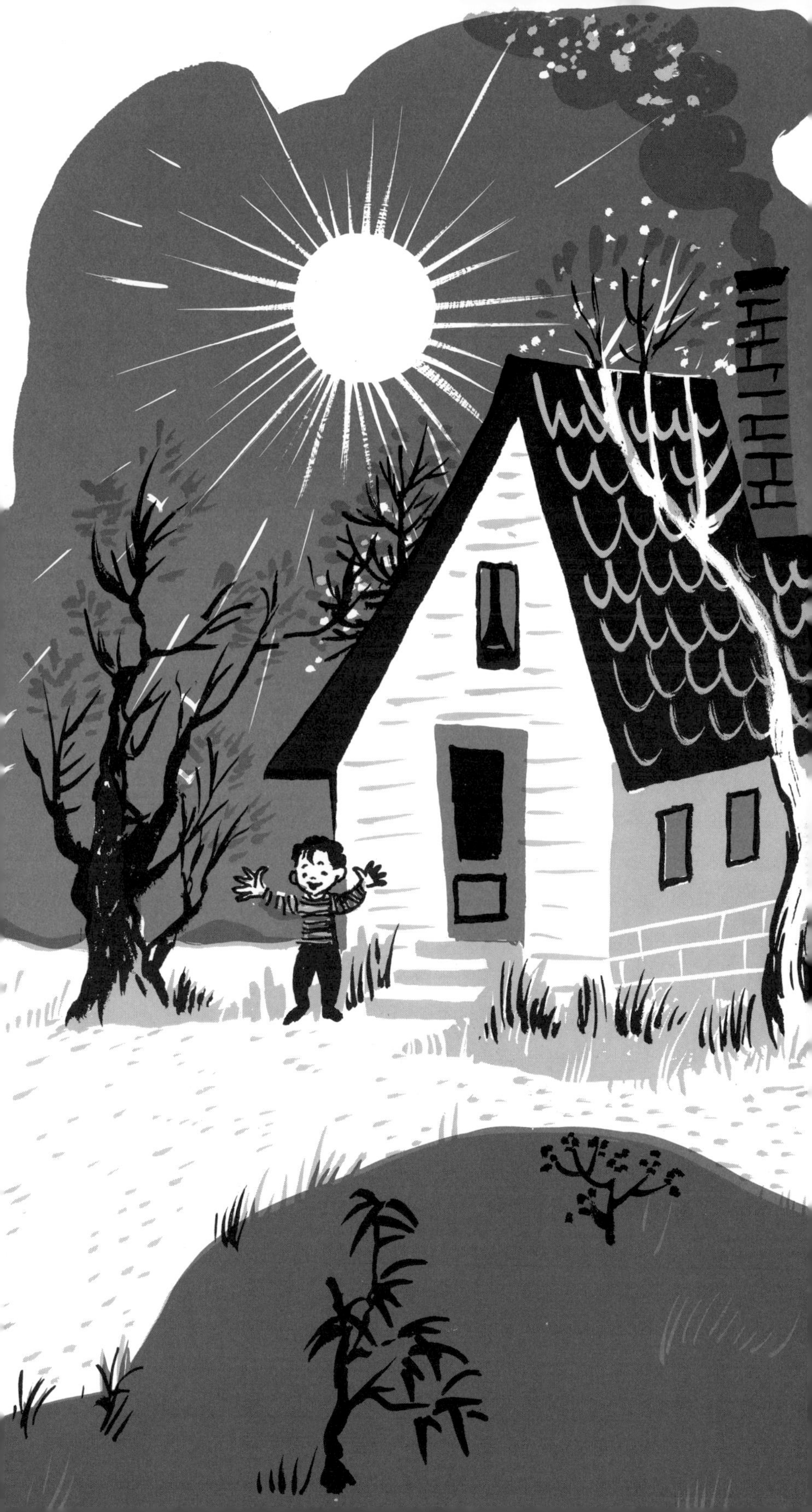

Mother cleans the house
until it shines like a mirror.

Mother cooks the special dinner
 we eat before Yom Kippur.

Everything must be finished
 before it's dark outside.
When it's dark, the fast begins,
 the time when *nobody* eats.

We eat a good dinner
>a big dinner
>>before our Yom Kippur fast.
After supper, Mother lights the candles.
The prayer takes longer than before Shabbat,
>because she makes a Yom Kippur wish
>for Daddy,
>>for David,
>>>and for me,
>because she makes a special wish
>>for her whole family.

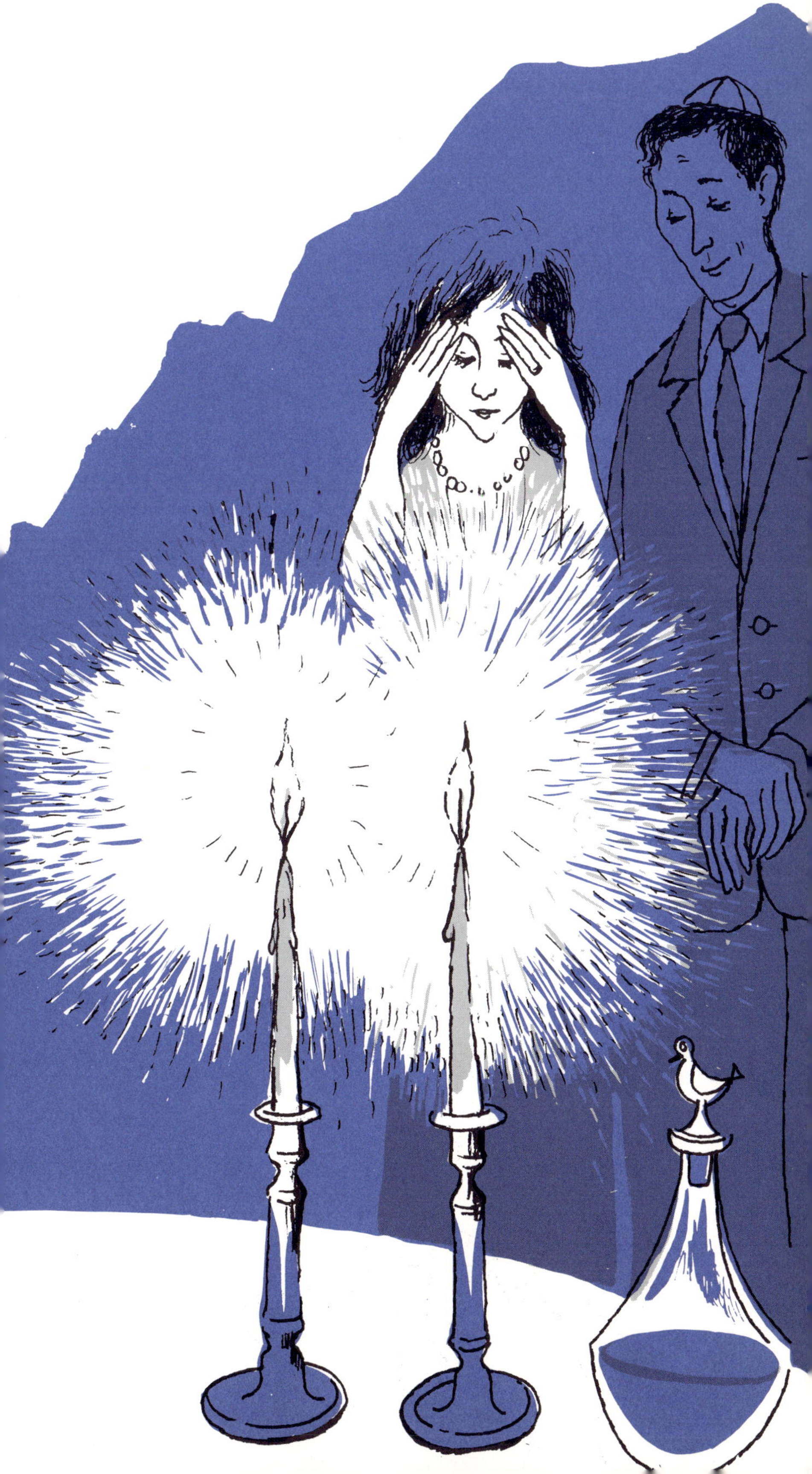

When I am a mother, I will know the prayer—

Barukh Atah Adonai, Elohenu Melekh Ha-Olam, Asher Kidshanu B'mitzvotav, V'tzivanu L'hadlik Ner Shel Yom Ha-Kippurim.

Barukh Atah Adonai, Elohenu Melekh Ha-Olam, Sheheḥeyanu Vikimanu V'higi'anu Lazman Hazeh.

יום הכפורים

להדליק נר של

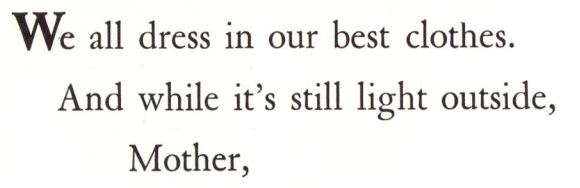

We all dress in our best clothes.
And while it's still light outside,
Mother,
Daddy,
David,
and I go to synagogue.
We go to hear the cantor sing
a special prayer.

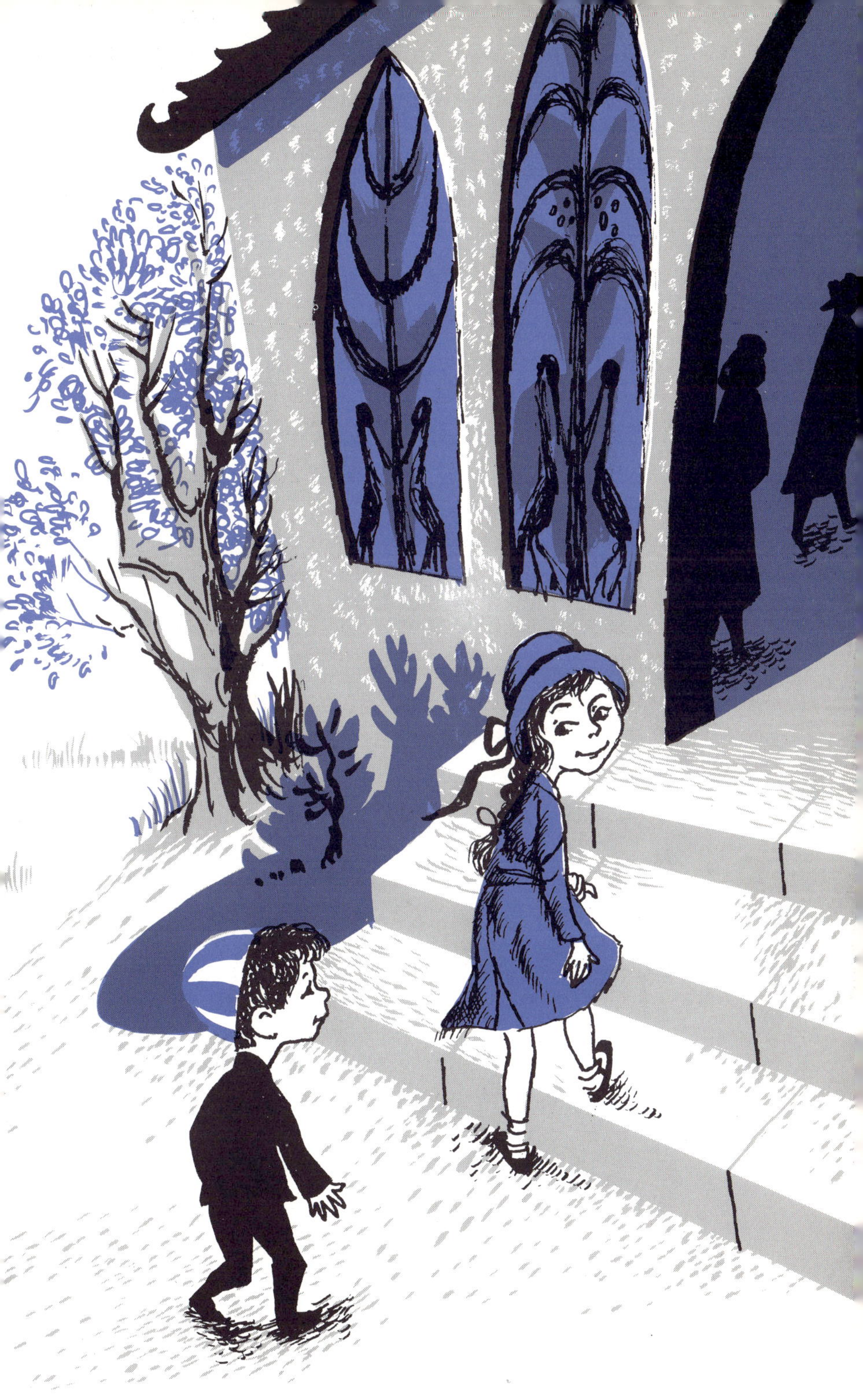

My daddy puts his *Tallit* on.
Yom Kippur is the only time
 every man wears a *Tallit* at night.
Yom Kippur is the only time
 our rabbi and our cantor dress in white.
Everyone is quiet.

Our Synagogue is full.
So many people, such a quiet place,
    such a long, long night.
When the sun goes down
    the cantor sings *Kol Nidre,*
    a special Yom Kippur prayer.

When we leave the synagogue,
 the sky is very dark.
Our candles at home are all burned down.
It's time for bed for David and for me.
We have no treat Yom Kippur night.
David and I are fasting.

Mother and Daddy fast tomorrow, too,
because Yom Kippur is a day to pray,
a day to stay in the synagogue.

In the morning
all the mothers and the fathers,
all the grandmothers and the grandfathers,
go to synagogue to stay all day.

It's too hard for children to fast all day.
The children go home for lunch.

When the sun is setting in the sky,
and the clouds are rosy red,
the *Shofar* blows one long blast—
long, loud, high.
The last *Shofar* blow of the High Holidays.

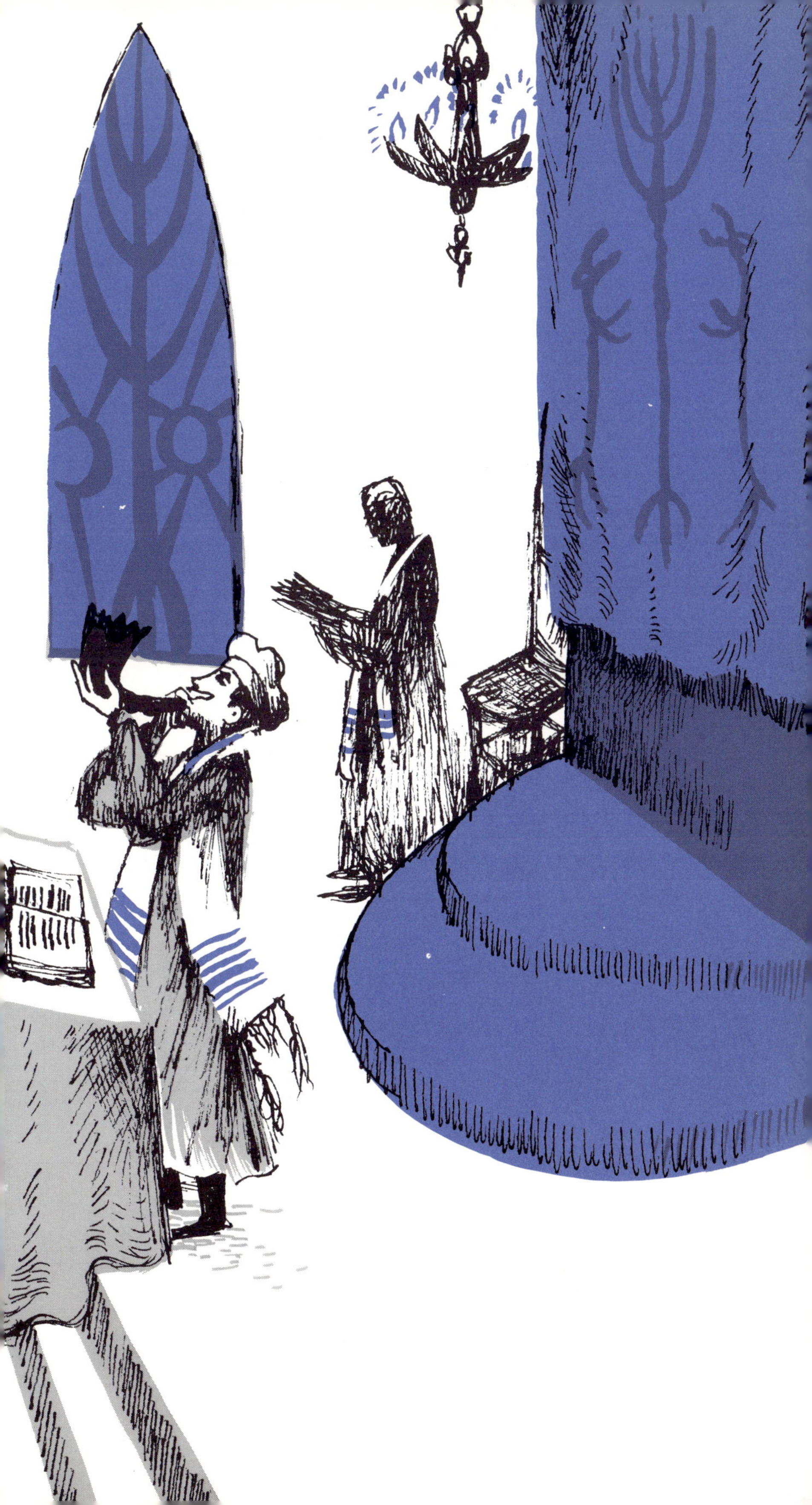

Every man takes off his *Tallit*
>and puts his prayer book away.

The grownups all shake hands
>and smile at each other.

They all say,
>"*Shanah Tovah,* Happy New Year."

The rabbi wishes everyone a happy New Year.
"Shanah Tovah," he says to David and to me.
He pats us both on the head.
I run around to talk to my friends
    after such a long quiet time.
I run around to all my friends.
"Shanah Tovah, Shanah Tovah,
    Shanah Tovah to you."

Mother,
   Daddy,
      David,
         and I come home from
            the synagogue.

Mother's very hungry,
   and Daddy's very hungry,
      when they end their fast
         after Yom Kippur day.

Fasting is over and eating begins
after Yom Kippur Day.
"Best chicken soup you ever made,"
Daddy tells my mother.
"Best noodles you ever made,"
David tells my mother.
Mother smiles and we all laugh.
We all feel happy together.
We all kiss each other.
We all say, *"Shanah Tovah."*
We begin our happy New Year.

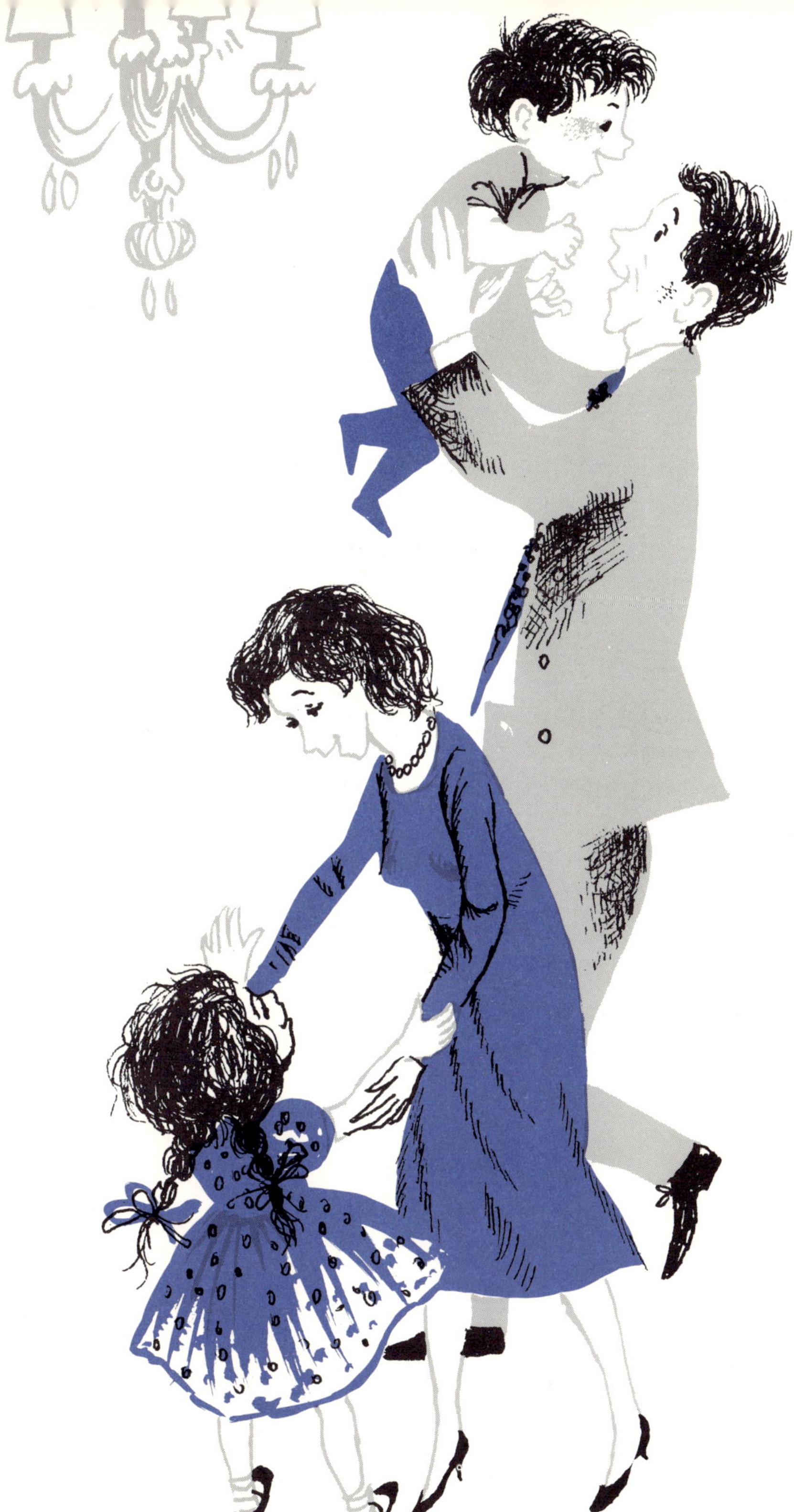